T0137689

Breaking Down Barriers

Breaking Down Barriers

Shirley Jones

To order additional copies of this book, contact:
Xlibris Corporation
1-888-795-4274
www.Xlibris.com
Orders@Xlibris.com
39921

CONTENTS

Thank You

It is times like this, that make me remember the life situations and events that have gotten me to where I am today. I would like to take this opportunity to send my utmost and heart filled Thank You to everyone that has supported and prayed for me. For which without, this book would not have been possible. I would like to send a loving Thank You to my husband Carl Jones, my children, friends & The Feet that Preach dance Ministry. And last but not least, I would like to send out a special thank you to Ms. Xanthe Bain.

Breaking Down the Barriers

Through Praise and Worship!

Preface

The truths and experiences recorded in this book have literally *torn* down the *walls* of doubt, fear, and unbelief in my life. They have given me freedom of expression and opened my eyes to see and experience God move as I dance through life.

Dance has given me joy unspeakable; nothing can compare. When I dance unto the Lord, my mind, soul, and body are transformed; and I feel renewed in my spirit. A time to be refreshed!

Trust the lord with all your heart and lean not to your own understanding, in all your ways acknowledge him and he will lead, and direct your path (Prov. 3:5-6).

These words I will always regard in my heart; it is a promise from the Lord. God is able to do exceedingly abundantly above all I could ever ask or think, so I trust him completely. My desire as you read this book is that you are blessed.

Praise and worship are mutually cooperative activities and similar in the way they are outwardly expressed, but they are not one and the same; each has its own nature and purpose.

Some churches are very vocal in their praise, but quite withdrawn when it comes to worship; while for others, it's easier to praise and enter into a sweetness of worship, but they have not yet learned the dynamics of praise and worship.

The Essence of Praise

Praise is not a difficult concept to understand for it is part of our everyday lives. We praise our children, we praise our husbands or wives, employers praise their employees, and so on; but above all that, praise is something we direct to God.

We praise God in a twofold manner.

1. We praise God directly by extolling him or expressing our admiration to him.
2. We praise God indirectly by commending him or magnifying him to others. Praise is preoccupied with who God is and his mighty acts.

God alone is worthy to be praised solely for who he is.

So then, praise can be directed to God or be expressed to others in reference to God.

How Is Praise Characterized?

Praise is characterized by celebration and is expressed through singing, shouting, speaking forth, playing musical instruments, dancing, and other external ways.

To merely contemplate the wonders of God is not entering into praise; meditation is not praise. Praise begins with a mind-set, but those thoughts must be put into action in order to qualify as praise.

Praise Is an Action Word

We have some folks in the church, and they're lovely people who fold their arms, lower their heads, purse their lips together, and say, "This is my way of praising God." Wrong! I firmly agree with Mr. Dutch Sheets when he says, there is no such thing as praising God in your own way. There is only God's way, and it is shown clearly to us in the scriptures.

"Let the sound of his praise be heard" (Ps. 66:8).

Pay close attention to this statement: Praise is not praise until it is vocalized or shown forth. In other words, it's impossible to praise God with your mouth shut and the body slumped over. With that posture, one might be worshipping or praying or even sleeping, but definitely not praising.

Praising God demands a response!

Demonstration of Praise

Now there are both vocal and nonvocal forms of praise, but whatever form of praise is demonstrated, others can clearly see the aspect of praise taking place.

Some of us are afraid to lift our voices for fear that someone might hear us; but fear is of the devil. Remember, we were created to make God's praise glorious. God has not given us the spirit of fear (see 2 Tim. 1:7). God's praises are not restricted to those with fine voices; if you can't sing it, speak it, dance it!

For those who are mute, who cannot speak, God's praise can still be shown forth in their countenance and bodily expressions; they praise in their spirit. We will never grow and mature in our expressions of praise until we are willing to praise God in a pleasing and authentic manner.

Praise Him in the Congregation

God places importance on praise in the congregation of the saints.

He seems to take pleasure in our congregated praise.

"Bless the Lord, oh my soul; and all that is with in me, bless His holy name" (Ps. 103). We will get many beneficial results when we praise God in the great congregation, but the Lord is pleased with unity and a variety of characteristics of congregational worship.

Why Praise?

The author Terry Law wrote a book entitled *Praise Releases Faith;* this book was very instrumental in my walk through faith. I was able to see the hand of God move in my life like never before. The spirit of God stirred inside my very soul and told me to just simply trust God. Faith is released when we praise God in advance for what he's getting ready to do. Trust and faith go hand in hand; the latter precedes the former—meaning, *faith is trust in action.*

Why praise? Because God inhabits the praises of his people. Our praise becomes the very throne of God, allowing him to sit in our midst and bless us according to our individual and corporate needs. God lives in our praise!

Psalm 150 says, "Let everything that hath breath praise the Lord." It is a command of the Lord to those whom he created in his image and likeness. An artist wrote a song that included the line "We were created to make God's praise glorious." Praising God is a command, but it is not something we always feel like doing.

Hebrew 13:15 reads, "By him therefore let us offer unto him a sacrifice of praise." *Sacrifice*—a word that demands a response, simply because the Lord deserves it. Do good and share with others, for with such sacrifice, God is well pleased.

Continual Praise

"I will bless the Lord at all times and his praises shall continually be in my mouth" (Ps. 34).

Continually is a powerful word that says, "Though He slay me, yet will I trust Him" (Job 13:15). Nothing broken. *I will myself to praise God continually*, despite what my eyes may see or what my ears may hear. *I will bless the Lord!*

There was a season in my life when I did not understand the transition that was taking place. Being married for the second time, my desire was to make it work.

In my prayer, I made my request known unto God by telling him what to do for my husband. "Make this man the way I want him to be right now." Big mistake!

It never dawned on me that my prayer was missing something very vital: *the will of the Father, not only in my prayer, but also in me.*

Marriage is honorable in the sight of God. When considering marriage, one must acknowledge God and be prepared to wait, receive, and respond according to his Word, which may or may not be the answer one desires. The most important thing for any marriage should be to honor God *continually* throughout a married couple's lives together (see Heb.4:12). When we yield our will to his, we become at peace with the results because we realize that in our struggle against sin (own selfish will), we have not resisted to the point of shedding our blood.

Through this, I've learned to always acknowledge God first before I do anything, trusting that whatever the answer will be, I'm in a susceptible mind-set to can all I get and get all I can. According to Proverbs 3:5-6, we must "trust in the Lord" always, knowing that he will lead and direct our path. This knowing is not in your head, it's in your spirit.

Sometimes in a marriage, you have disagreements and personal differences, views, likes, and dislikes. In those times, because the arguments often get very heated, you want out. Because of the heat, you make spontaneous decisions that bring long-term results.

We never stop to think or walk away because everyone wants to have the last word. Things get out of hand, and you say things that hurt, and it takes a while to get to a place of recovery. But when we pray, we must consider our ways and our words. Our words must line up with the will of the Father, and we must learn how to want to do his will. Always keep in mind that our marriage, as well as everything else, must honor God.

After considering your ways, the first step to recovery is learning how to apologize. Give up your will and allow the will of the Father to manifest in you; seek him with your whole heart. Scripture records that "there is no want to those who diligently seek him." When we pray, whether it be for our marriage, children, jobs, friends, ministries, or just relationships, we must find out what the Word says about it, speak it more than you believe, but you must first believe.

I remember attending a women's conference at Without Walls International Church. Pastor Darlene Bishop was the speaker that night, and she said that the Lord ministered to her the word *believe,* and the revelation she got from that was this: "Because Emmanuel lives, I have victory every time." If any man comes to Christ, he must first believe that he is rewarder of them that diligently seek him.

Praise His Name

Psalms 149:1-3 says,

> Praise ye the Lord. Sing unto the Lord a new song, and his praise in the
>
> congregation of saints.
>
> Let Israel rejoice in him that made him: let the children of Zion be joyful
>
> in their King.
>
> Let them praise his name in the dance: let them sing praises unto him with
>
> the timbrel and harp.

The second book of Corinthians 9:7 says, "The Lord loves a cheerful giver." When we think of this scripture, we usually think tithes and offerings, never considering that when we give anything unto the Lord, we must have a cheerful attitude; so this passage clearly speaks of our attitude in our giving.

Let's look closer at Psalms 149. Here we have a twofold purpose: In reach and Out reach. In reaching in, we, the people of God, are edified (Ps. 149:1-6). In reaching out, we draw (Ps. 149:7-9).

Praise is powerful! We must not underestimate the voice we have. When our voice is lined up with faith and purpose, the Word of God becomes sharper than any two-edged sword and brings into captivity every thought and everything so that they are in obedience of Christ, the Anointed One, and are his for anointing.

The anointing destroys the yokes and removes every burden. The word being joined with *faith* is *mighty*. The Lord takes pleasure when we operate by faith; it pleases him.

When we allow God to be God in our lives, we learn his nature and his names.

Praise the Names of God!

Names, References, and Descriptions

ADONAI (Isa. 6:1)

> The owner and ruler of everything.

ELOHIM (Gen. 1:1)

> The All-Powerful Creator and Promise Keeper.

EL SHADDAI (Gen. 17:1)

> he Almighty One who nourishes, satisfies, and supplies.

EL ROI (Gen. 16:13)

> The Almighty One who sees us.

JEHOVAH (Exod. 3:14)

> The only self-existent everlasting God.

JEHOVAH-JIREH (Gen. 22:14)

> The One who sees my needs and shall provide.

JEHOVAH-NISSI (Exod. 17:15)

> Our banner, our flag of victory.

JEHOVAH-M'KIDDESH (Exod. 31:13)

> The Lord who sanctifies us, makes us holy.

JEHOVAH-ROPHE (Exod. 15:26)

> The Lord who heals, restores, and cures.

JEHOVAH-ROHI (Ps. 23:1)

> The Lord is our Shepherd.

JEHOVAH-SABBAOTH (2 Sam. 6:2)

> The Lord of Hosts.

JEHOVAH-SHALOM (Judg. 6:24)

    The Lord is our peace.

JEHOVAH-SHAMMAH (Ezek. 46:35)

    The Lord is here.

JEHOVAH-TSIDKENU (Jer. 23:5-6)

    The Lord is our righteousness.

Remember that Jesus said, "I and the Father are One" (John 10:30). These names signify Jesus as well as the Father.

There are still many other names that I have not mentioned. The apostle Paul said, "Oh that I might know him, get to know him for yourself! Praise his name and sing unto the Lord a new song."

Enter into His gates with thanksgiving and into His courts with praise (Psalm 100:4).

Praise can unlock the gates to freedom. Praise is the key that allows you to enter the inner courts and the Holy of Holies (the presence of the Lord).

In the presence of the Lord, there is fullness of joy. The joy of the Lord is our strength! The strength of the Lord is the presence of the Lord in you and in your person making *you strong in the Lord and in the power of his might!*

Our desire should be to remain in him, make him our sanctuary; there "shall no evil befall thee neither any plague come nigh thy dwelling" (Ps. 91:9-10). His presence becomes our secret place where we offer up our praise and worship.

No wonder the Word says, "Put on the garment of praise for the spirit of heaviness." Praise is a garment of armor that the believer can always wear without being weighted down. The weight comes before the praise with the spirit of heaviness.

With the right attitude, we are able to lay aside every weight and rise above our situation and/or circumstances to a level of expectancy.

Right attitude determines our altitude!

We are exhorted to praise God's name in the dance and praise him with musical instruments and dance (Ps. 149:3, 150:4).

Worship involves obedience, preparation, separation, and sacrifice unto the Lord

"God is a Spirit and they that worship him must worship in spirit and in truth" (John 4:24). In this passage, Jesus emphasizes that true worship stems from the inside outward; it is a matter of the heart. We worship when we know the Word and experience Jesus through obedience.

Henry Blackaby wrote the book *Experiencing God*. In it he spoke about seven realities.

1. God is always at work around you.
2. God pursues a continuing love relationship that is real and personal.
3. God invites you to become involved with him in his work.
4. God speaks by the Holy Spirit, through the Bible by the Holy Spirit, prayer, circumstances, and the church to reveal himself, his purpose, and his ways.

5. God's invitation for you to work with him always brings you to a crisis of belief that requires faith and action.

6　You must make major adjustments in your life to join God in what he's doing.

7. You come to know God by experience as you obey him and he accomplish his work through you.

Worship is tied up with sacrifice.

　　　Abraham offered up his son Isaac (Gen. 22:7-10).

　　　Hannah gave her son (1 Sam. 1:27-28).

To worship means to give up something to God. He is "worthy to receive power and riches and wisdom and strength and honor, glory and blessings" (Rev. 5:12).

The Bible tells us in Romans 12:1 to "present your bodies as a living sacrifice."

Holy living is a sacrifice, and it is acceptable to God always.

Aspect of Worship

*A*spect is a noun that means an outward appearance, look, or direction a thing faces. We praise until worship comes and we worship until the Glory comes.

Entrance Level No. 1
Tabernacle: Order

Outer-Court Praise

Inner-Court Worship

Holy of Holies: Glory

Entrance Level No. 1
Praise

Praise is to esteem or command, to speak of approval or admiration, to applaud, to glorify God.

Worship is a noun which means "to revere," "pay homage to," "to kiss God," and "lifestyle."

Neokoros, a Greek word, is translated as "worshipper" and as "the act of bowing down in homage, generally done before a superior or a ruler."

Shachah is a Hebrew word that means "to prostrate oneself" or "to bow down."

Eliezer, Abraham's servant, "bowed down his head and worshiped the Lord" (Gen. 24:26).

Moses "bowed his head toward the earth and worshiped" (Exod. 34:8) when God came down and stood with him on Mt. Sinai.

Ezra, the reformer, blessed the Lord, "All the people answered Amen, Amen, with Lifting up their hands: and they bowed their heads, and worshiped the Lord with their faces to the ground" (Neh. 8:6).

The psalmist exhorts us to, "O come, let us worship and bow down: let us kneel before the Lord our Maker" (Psalm 95:6).

Sahah is a Greek word used as the common term for coming before God in worship (1 Sam. 15:25, Jer. 7:2).
Sometimes this is in conjunction with another Hebrew verb for bowing down physically followed by worship as in Exodus 34:8.

Entrance Level No. 2
Worship: Coming Clean

Place or hold a clean white handkerchief out away from you. From the distance, you are unable to see the spots on that handkerchief; but as you get closer, you will find that there are still spots there even though initially the handkerchief was thought to have been clean.

When we are in God's presence, the aspect of worship is to bow down and fall prostrate before him for God alone is holy. With tears streaming down your face, you experience God's stroke of love upon you. Glory to Jesus!

We cry, "Abba, cleanse us!" God already knows where we are, so he invites us to come. We yield, agreeing with him that we need to be cleansed. I come clean, so I become clean because of the consuming fire. In times of iniquity, sin is burned up by sacrifice. Something is given up, sacrifice becomes a sweet-smelling savior unto the Lord!

Tabernacle Level No. 3
Glory

The Glory manifested at the time you get to know the Lord of the work. He speaks and invites us when he's already at work, preparing us for the work of the Lord.

He's Preparing Me
Consecration and Dedication

Romans 12:1-2 says, "Present your bodies as a living sacrifice holy and acceptable unto God which is our reasonable service," meaning it's the least we can do considering all his benefits towards us.

What Are the Benefits?

Knowing and experiencing God's love, forgiveness, redemption, salvation, righteousness, grace, mercy, Holy Spirit, and power; being heirs; having access into the heavens; building ourselves up on our most holy faith; goodness, joy, peace, long-suffering, temperance, meekness, greatness, his image, likeness and being his expressed personality here on the earth; and so much more!

As a dancer, one must be set apart (Num. 16:26; Isa. 52:11).

Not only dancers, but anyone called to a specific work in the ministry. These passages of scripture speak of being called to separate ourselves from the world. Be in the world, but not of the world. We must see ourselves as God see us—holy, different, unique, and being a light to those in darkness. The lifestyle of a spirit-filled dancer should reflect God his kingdom and his mightiness. Worship is a lifestyle (see John 4:24). We reflect God through the way we live, the music we listen to, the types of dances we do, and the garments we wear.

Everything we do must bring honor to God!

Levitical Dancers / Joined Dancers

Levi means joined

Levitical dancers must have one mind, one purpose—unity.

Everything begins with prayer. Prayer enables you to become more intimate with God. Prayer is also our source of spiritual growth, God's forgiveness, faith building, and Christ's guidance. There are key principles to prayer according to Mathew 6:6-7:

1. Enter into your closet.
2. Shut the door.
3. Pray to the Father.
4. Use not vain repetition.

Sweet Hour of Prayer: Being Cleansed from Known Sin

"I acknowledge my sin to thee, and my iniquity I did not hide; I said I will confess my transgressions to the Lord, and thou did'st forgive the guilt of my sin, this comes before going forth" (Ps. 32:5).

What Is Sin?

Sin is whatever

1. weakens your reason,
2. impairs the readiness of your conscience,
3. obscures your sense of God,
4. takes away the relish for spiritual things,
5. and increases the strength and authority of your body over your mind.

Your mind is the throne of God, It is your heart. Listen. If God can't be in what you're doing, don't do it.

Movement and expressions come from within, and your life must be a living epistle. If you're walking in bitterness, jealousy, or any other work of the flesh, you should not dance (1Sam. 18:5-9; Song of Sol. 8:6).

Not only can God not use you while you're walking in bitterness, he won't use you because of *impartation*, which means "to give or share something," "make known," or "to communicate." Operating in bitterness will cause great harm to the body. In order for God to use you as a catalyst, you must go through the cleansing process.

Impartation of the wrong spirits will prevent the body from being blessed.
Never be so self-conscious that you forget to be God's conscience.
Desire the impartation of the anointing. Dance should bring unity.
The Jewish people danced a dance called Machol; this was a dance of unity.
The dance signified a covenant, an agreement by the holding of the hands. Same movement, same God, same focus, same purpose.

What Should My Purpose Be?

Purpose should be to bring the focus of the congregation to worship.

Purpose and Destiny

Jeremiah 29:11 says, "For I know the thoughts that I think towards You, saith the Lord, thoughts of peace, and not of evil, to give you an expected end."

Zephaniah 3:17 says, Jesus is the Lord of the dance and every good and perfect gift comes from the Lord. So giving back to the Maker is the least we can do.

Praise Posture and Purpose

Praise posture is a language that is visual and necessary.

Praise Postures

SING UNTO THE LORD (Ps. 33:3)

CLAP YOUR HANDS (Ps. 47:1)

PRAISE WITH MY WHOLE HEART (Ps. 9:1)

PRAISE THEE WITH JOYFUL LIPS (Ps. 63:5)

TREAD UPON SERPENTS AND SCORPIONS (Luke 10:19)

FEET THAT PRAECH (Rom. 10:17)

LIFT UP HOLY HANDS (2 Sam. 6:14)

DANCE (Exod. 15:20)

BOW DOWN (Rom. 14:11)

Because of who God is.

Seven Words of Praise

Yadah

Yadah is a verb with a root meaning "the extended hand"; "to throw out the hand" (see also 2 Chron. 20:21; Ps. 63:1).

Halal

Halal is a primary root word for praise; our word *hallelujah* comes from this base word. It means "to be clear," "to shine," "to boast, show," "to rave," "to celebrate," "to be clamorously foolish" (Ps. 150:1; Ps. 149:3).

Towdah

Towdah comes from the same principle as *yadah*, but used more specifically, it refers to an extension of the hand in adoration, acceptance (Ps. 50:14; Ps. 50:23).

Barak

Barak means "to kneel down," "to bless God as an act of adoration" (Psalm 95:6; Ps. 34:1).

Shabach

Shabach means "to shout," "to address in a loud tone," "to command," "to triumph" (Ps. 145:4; Isa. 12:6).

Zamar

Zamar means "to pluck the strings of an instrument," "to sing," "to praise," "musical word" (Ps. 21:13; Ps. 57:8-9).

Karar

This word means "to whirl or to move in a circle, to dance wildly" (2 Sam. 6:14).

Liturgical Dance

Dance is a ministry, which makes us ministers; and as ministers, we must be able to communicate. Pride can keep one from going forth. God hates pride, so if you find yourself more concerned about what people think, rather than what God thinks of you, you are operating on pride. Pride is a spirit that needs to be broken. To flow as a dancer, it is important that you learn how to communicate effectively. Learn how to let go of anything and everything that could hinder you by going through the cleansing process. Keep yourself planted deep in Jesus and learn scriptures in order to meditate. Four years ago, I attended a dance camp in Orlando, Florida. Dr. E. Harriston was the speaker. "I call her the mother of liturgical dance," she said, as she spoke about the seasons of ministry and the seasons in our life. She said, "If you don't move when God says, 'Move,' you will miss your season." She went on to say that during the winter it's usually cold and you find yourself alone even when you're in a room full of people. In the spring, things begin to bloom. During this time, you flourish, ministry begins to grow, and it's time to go forth. In the summer, things get very hot. You find yourself going through fiery trials, which can sometimes cause you to think strangely and almost melt down. But you have to remember that the trials came to make you strong. In the fall, the leaves fall from the trees. This is a time for separation. A time when you separate yourself from people, places, and things. It's called a time of consecration. We must learn the times and seasons of ministry and life itself and be prepared to meet God wherever he is already at work.

In simplicity, learn when to move and when not to move; it will make the difference in whether or not you miss or experience your season. Dance is a very vital part of the worship service. It is not separate, it is an intricate part. Many times in the worship service, the dancers don't communicate; they just dance. Being a dancer, whether you're a praise dancer or prophetic dancer, even in spontaneity you must understand communication. Make sure you're able to paint a portrait of the word. There's an old cliché that says, "A picture is worth a thousand words."

The people must be able to understand what you're saying through your interpretation. Many refer to dance as *interpretive dance* when done in the church, while others refer to all dances as *praise dance*. Many are not able to determine the difference between praise, prophetic, devotional, congregational, or spontaneous dance. They just surmise dance as being just dance. As a dancer, being able to communicate takes precedence over technique, over how high you can kick, or how high you can leap; it's all about communication. Another factor that is vitally important is that the dancer must communicate with his or her pastor. Knowing the heart of the pastor will help in the direction of prayer for the dancer, such as what music to choose and whether the lyrics will coincide with the message, or to just be ready to minister spontaneously when called or led.

The Qualifications of a Liturgical Dancer

1. Have a personal relationship with Jesus Christ.
2. Have a lifestyle conducive to that of a worshiper.
3. Maintain a daily devotion, prayer for personal life, for support, vision for ministry, and the souls of men.

4. Forsake not to assemble together with other believers; attend church regularly.

5. Be involved in Sunday school.

6. Have the right attitude, submission, and humility.

7. FAT, simply means to be faithful, accountable, and teachable.

8. Keeping oneself free from contaminated thoughts, words, or deeds.

9. Dress appropriately as representatives of Christ.

10. Be faithful in attendance for rehearsals and engagements.

The holistic purpose of the dancer is to bring the focus of the people to worship the Father; to edify, to impart whatever is needed to the body; to inspire the people to *kiss* God daily; to break up the fallow ground, making the heart ready to receive the Word of God, which means less work for the pastor; and to make sure the dance movement makes sense.

Remember, everything we do must bring honor to God, so our motive must be pure!

Priestly Garments (Exod. 28:1-43)

The purpose of priestly garments is for beauty and glory: the symbol of bringing *dignity and honor* to the name of God!

The Call of the Priest

1. *A robe

2. *A woven tunic

3. *A turban: the source of the call from God

4. *The purpose of the call: to set the priest apart from all other people

5. *The symbol of the High Priest's special call: to stir dignity and honor for God's call

Skilled people were appointed to make the special garments.

Garments consisted of the following:

1. * A chest piece or breast piece

2. * An ephod

3. * Belt

4. * Linen under garment

The Purpose for Each Piece

Ephod and stones. The priest represents and carries the name of God's people before the Lord.

Chest piece. The priest represents and carries the names of God's people upon his heart and he represents them before the Lord continually.

The urim and thummim. Two stones next to the high priest's heart symbolize the high priest seeking God's will for the people.

The robe of the ephod. Long sleeveless solid blue robe symbolizes that the people must seek the acceptance of the Holy God.

Final instruction governing the clothing. To set them apart for dignity and respect.

Linen under garments. Clothing from waist to thigh is for modesty and purity.

*   *The Priest is to be clothed in the garments then ordained.*

Modesty: to cover their nakedness

Purity: to keep from arousing God's anger and judgment against immodesty and immorality

The more you wear, the less you bare!

The garments we wear as priestly dancers must reflect God's kingdom and mightiness.

Getting Started

Prayer is the key. The heart and vision are the doors. Knowing the vision of the church and the heart of your pastor is essential. You must get all you can of the can-all-you-get by attending workshops, seminars, and dance camps. Doing so will help to enhance ministry and build you up as a minister.

Learn how to listen to music and allow the Holy Spirit to dictate movement that will be powerful and effective in communicating the message. Read 2 Chronicles 15:14-22. Make sure music is able to minister. The words must be clear, and you must be able to dance to it. Not all music can be translated into movement. If it doesn't fit, don't force it! When choosing music, listen to it several times and allow the Holy Spirit to suggest movement to you. You may have to listen several times before doing so. Make sure the one who is in charge of the music is skillful. This is very important because you don't want someone who does not know or understand what you want or the importance of cueing the music just right.

Any cracked wrong song and starting the music too late can cause the anointing to go or stop the quenching of the spirit and break the flow of the anointing.

During these times, someone may be ready to receive and the Holy Spirit has convicted their heart; then all of a sudden, a loud sound, screech, or crack, or a long pause in the flow of the service, could prevent that person from coming forth or yielding to the

Holy Spirit. To help in your understanding, read also 2 Chronicles 20:21. There were a group of people many years back, known as the Shakers, who were from Europe, and their shaking movement was a part of their worship service. Slavery brought problems with the dance—because the slaves knew and understood the power of the dance but the masters did not. The interesting thought about that is this: When we don't understand or don't want to do something, we find fault with it. Then we question it and ultimately try to get rid of it.

Be careful how you present yourselves as ministers.

You don't want your goodness to be spoken of as evil. As a representative of Christ, we must learn what is good and acceptable unto God, and when we do this, he will make your enemies behave.

Being skilled at what you do only makes you more effective!
We are to skillfully praise God!
Wisdom is applied knowledge. Understanding is the principal thing.
Get wisdom and understanding, but above all, get the skill.

Choreography

When choreographing, never use too much hip movement and always consider the words of the song, which has to make sense through movement. Music and movement have levels, and as a good listener, you must determine when to change, build up, or soften the movement. Watch carefully to see the ability of each dancer, this helps with placement, meaning you're able to see their strengths and weaknesses. Just as a music director will place a strong soprano next to a weak soprano to balance and help with voice execution, the choreographer must do the same with the dancers and use them where they are most effective.

For instance, if you have a dancer who loves to jump or leap or do splits, allow him or her to go to that area when needed. If a person likes to do turns, or if they are the graceful type who executes movement well and gracefully, allow him or her to go forth. This will give you a strong, well-balanced group, and everyone will be more appreciative and supportive of one another. This will help build relationships among the dancers for as they dance, they flow. Why?

No issues!

Make sure every dancer has the proper garments needed for ministry. Vitally important, because when you go forth, everyone must be in accord. Same movement, same garment, unless otherwise suggested for better interpretation by the choreographer.

Respect the choreographer or director's suggestions!

The choreographer is the visionary of the dance ministry, and without a vision, the people will perish; so pray for your leaders always. (*Just do it!*)

Thinking always of purpose, this is I, not the Lord, personally feel that one must consider the message one is trying to send when ministering.

1. Never wear flashy nail polish on long nails. Doing so will only bring attention to you and not to God.
2. Never keep hairstyles that are very flamboyant, no braids. These will also bring attention to you and not to God.

3. Never wear lipsticks or liner that are not appropriate or complementary; for instance, never wear black liner on lips. Lips should be stained with a medium brown or an appropriate color pencil.

4. Always wear proper undergarments. Make sure everyone has white, black, and nude leotards and tights.

5. Personal hygiene must be implemented always as this will prevent offensive odors.

6. Feet must be cared for also and polish can be used, just make sure they're soft colors and not too flashy.

7. Learn how to apply makeup properly as you want to always look nice. Proper application can enhance or minimize unwanted features.

8. Always wear small post earrings, no excessive jewelry.

9. Allow God to use every pain and hurt to do a greater work.

Working in you is his will while you work out your soul for salvation with fear and trembling, allowing others to see your good work, and glorify the Father.

These things may not seem important, but they are; and as a dancer, discipline takes precedence over desire. As you exercise discipline, you begin to possess the fruit of the spirit called self-control, in which there is no such law.

Turning Up the Heat

To help turn up the heat in the worship service, you can use, flags, banners, streamers, handkerchiefs, and more. There are many ways you can minister unto the Lord. Praise and worship causes participation. Getting the people involved in the service is the most important thing.

Participation promotes anticipation, so we wait with joyful expectations for the Lord to bless his people through faith impartation.

When the heat is turned up, everyone's bands will be loose, and you will see things begin to drop off in the spirit realm and the people begin to worship.

We do not have to limit ourselves in our expressions to God because there is so much that we need from him. We seek avenues to express our love and gratitude toward him. Knowing and understanding biblical forms of expressions will enable dancers, musicians, and worship leaders to tap into season, purpose, and destiny.

That's an awesome view!

Breaking Down the Barriers

Through Praise and Worship!

Praise—Worship, mutually cooperative activities and are similar

in the way they are outwardly expressed, but they are not one and the

same, each has it's own nature and purpose.

Some churches are very vocal in their praise, but quite withdrawn

when it comes to worship. While for others it's easier to praise

and enter into a sweetness in worship, but have not yet learned the

dynamics of praise and worship.

THE ESSENCE OF PRAISE

Praise is not a difficult concept to understand, for it is part of our everyday

lives. We praise our children, we praise our husbands/wives, employers

praise their employees and so on, but above all that praise is something

we direct to God.

We praise God in a two-fold manner.

1. We praise God directly by extolling him or expressing our admiration to him.

2. We praise God indirectly by commending him or magnifying him to others
   Praise is preoccupied with who God is, and his mighty acts.

God alone is worthy to be praised solely for who he is.

So then praise can be direct to God, or be expressed to others in reference to God.

How is praise characterized? Praise is characterized by celebration and is expressed through singing, shouting, speaking forth, playing musical instruments, dancing and other external ways.

To merely contemplate the wonders of God has not entered into praise, meditation is not praise. Praise begin with a mind set, but those thoughts must be put into action in order to qualify as praise.

PRAISE IS AN ACTION WORD

We have some folk in the church, and they're lovely people who fold their arms, lower their heads and purse their lips together and say this is my way of praising God. "WRONG! I firmly agree with Mr. Dutch Sheets when he say's, there is no such thing as praising God in your own way! There's only Gods way and they are shown clearly to us in the scriptures.

psalm 66:8 Let the sound of his praise be heard.
Pay close attention to this statement, praise is not praise until it is vocalized or shown forth. In other words it's impossible to praise God with your mouth shut and the body slumped over.
With that posture one might be worshipping or praying or even sleeping, but definitely not praising.
Praising God demands a response!

DEMONSTRATION OF PRAISE

Now there are both vocal and non-vocal forms of praise, but whatever
form of praise is demonstrated, others can clearly see the aspect
of praise taking place.

Some of us are afraid to lift our voices, for fear that someone might
hear them, but fear is of the devil. Remember, we were created
to make God's praise glorious. (II Timothy 1:7) God has not given
us the spirit of fear, Gods praises are not restricted to those with fine
voices, if you can't sing it, speak it, dance it!

For those who are mute cannot speak, Gods praise can still be shown
forth in their countenance, and bodily expressions, they praise in their
spirit. We will never grow and mature in our expressions of praise until
we are willing to praise God in a pleasing and authentic manner.

PRAISE HIM IN THE CONGREGATION

Psalm 103:

God places importance on praise in the congregation of the saints.
He seems to take pleasure in our congregated praise. Psalm 34: say's
Bless the Lord oh my soul and all that is with in me, bless his holy
Name. We will get many beneficial results, when we praise God in the
great congregation, but the Lord is pleased with unity, and a variety of
characteristics of congregational worship.

The Holy Spirit inspires unity; we don't have to demand it. In other words, we do not need
to be pumped and primed. The incense used in the holy of holies of Moses's tabernacle

was compounded from several different fragrances in order to produce what God desired. Symbolically, this shows us that the variety of praises in the congregation is very pleasing to him. People may be standing or kneeling, others with their hands raised, others dancing, which may seem out of order, but it is orderly variety. The presence of the Lord is here when we are joined in our praise to him. Have you ever noticed how some people praise God as if they are out of their minds, or when they shout before the Lord, forgetting about everyone and everything around them? They can do this because their sacrifice has been great! The greater the sacrifice, the greater the praise!

Sacrifice—giving up something you thought you had to have because you love God more.

MAN

NO SACRIFICE   NO MIRACLE

NO PRAISE

Genesis chapter 20 speaks of God's divine order.

Pay close attention to this. Abraham had a son by his wife Sarah's handmaiden. He loved her and his son very much. God spoke to Abraham, telling him that he would be the father of many nations, through his seed and his wife Sarah's womb (order). The child began mocking Sarah (problem), so Abraham had to put the bondwoman and the child out (sacrifice); something he thought he had to have. The Lord told Abraham that the child would receive his portion. Today, we know this same portion to be "child support". The child was not God's choice, nor was he to be Abraham's heir. Abraham, the man, had to make a sacrifice—the child and bondwoman—in order for the miracle to take place, which was for the barren wife Sarah to give birth to the heir.

What Is Your Spiritual Act of Worship?

According to Mathew 2:2, astrologers, or the magi, came from the East to worship the one who was born as the King of the Jews. Worship is reverence or honor paid to God, ceremonies or services expressing such reverence, an utterly devoted admiration for a person, to be full of adoration, offering worship, and adoring. Romans 12:1 states, "I beseech you brethren by the mercies of God, that you present your bodies a living sacrifice holy and acceptable unto God." Holiness is an act of worship. The magi-astrologers, not as we know them today, were of the priestly tribe of Medes, experts of the stars who were searching for the god of stars. The magi symbolized the non-Jewish world and all who searched for ultimate truth.

Says I Chronicles 16:29, "Ascribe to the Lord the glory due his name gift. Bring an offering and come before him worship the Lord in the splendor of his holiness."
Giving is an act of worship.

Psalms 96:6-8 says, "Come, let us bow down in worship let us kneel before the Lord our make, for we are the people of his pasture the flock under his care."
Humility is an act of worship.

Ascribe to the Lord the glory due his name; bring an offering and come into his courts, meaning come into his presence offering a concrete expression of praise to God. Can we worship without giving? *The answer is no!*

Offerings can sometimes conjure up images of obligation like that of taxes and bills, but the word can also be translated as "gift," something we lovingly, cheerfully offer out of our gratitude to Christ who has given us everything. So giving gifts to God, then, is a necessary and natural part of true worship.

True praise prompts true worship and worship is a lifestyle.

Watch out for idols and images!

In what ways do people worship images? Psalm 97:7 says, "Confounded be all they that serve graven images, that boast themselves of idols: worship him all ye gods." We can begin to worship the knowledge of the word more than the word itself. Hebrews 1:6 says, "And again when he bringeth the first born into the world, he saith, AND LET ALL THE ANGELS OF GOD WORSHIP HIM." We're talking about Jesus, who, in the brightness of his glory and the expressed image of his person upheld all things by the power of his Word, the one who sat and is seated at the right hand of the Father after purging our sins, still making intercession for us; he's the Word made flesh, and he is the only one worthy of being worshipped.

We should boast only in the Lord. It is through him that we live, move, and define and complete our being. As the Holy Spirit reveals, so we are dealt with. Revelation then includes seeing and slaying. It is God's unique way of dealing with us. Once uncleanness is really exposed, it cannot remain. Scripture records, "God is light and in him there is no darkness at all." Therefore, light reveals and slays; it causes one to fall prostrate before him, and being slain by light is the most needful exposure and experience a believer could ever have. Why? Because light shows up whatever is there! Remember

Paul the apostle, on the road to Damascus and the experience he had? He did not walk to the side of the road and bow when the light shown upon him as he fell down. Paul reacted to the light by falling down; he was inwardly exposed. This happened all at once., God always shows us how polluted and wicked we are; how hateful, prideful, boastful, disgusting, and despicable we really and truly are; how we are such lovers of ourselves. And our response is always, "Alas! What a wretch I am." God reveals our true self, all for our own good; that is, we have to die so that we may gain. Remember, God resists the proud but give grace to the humble. This exposure of light is a time of enlightening and believing. The scriptures says, "If any man comes to the Lord, he must first believe that he is a rewarder." Accept the sentence of repentance and agree with his judgment for he is our judge. Listen! The more we wholeheartedly agree with the Word, the more we become ready for more light. The more light we receive, the more we become like him!

It says in 1 John 2:8-10, "Again, a new commandment I write unto you, Because the darkness is past, and the true light now shineth. He that saith he is in the light, and hateth his brother, is in darkness even until now. He that loveth his brother abideth in the light and there is none occasion of stumbling in him." Thank God for not leaving us alone; he keeps right on working on us, in us, and through us until we are totally bare before him. He knows where we are, and he knows the thoughts and intents of our hearts as he reveals to us ourselves; and there we are, bare, naked, and waiting for him to cover us with his wings of love. Through true worship, we see who and what we really are. We no longer think of ourselves highly than we ought to. We're ashamed to even show ourselves. We try to find words that will adequately describe us, but it's to no avail; we must fall at the feet of Jesus and repent. Such enlightening frees us from long years of bondage.

Breaking Down the Barriers

When the son has set free, he is free, indeed! This is a process of elimination. We must learn to stand in this liberty and be not entangled with the yokes of bondage. Christ has set us free!

This freedom breaks the outermost man, as well as the inner man, because of the anointing which removes burdens and destroys yokes. We become broken vessels; now, our innermost man can emerge. We are, then, led by the Spirit of God to do his perfect will and as a light to those who are in darkness. Worship is the process of elimination.

This process is the essence of true worship—pouring ourselves out before the Lord, allowing him to see the good and the bad his purifying and cleansing, so that we might enter into the most holy place.

Breaking Down Barriers

Let the Children Come!

Luke 18:16 says, "But Jesus called them unto him, and said, suffer the little children to come unto me, and forbid them not: for of such is the kingdom of God." God's people are to be those who celebrate life in the Lord. We should be free, joyous, and loving. We should be so in tune with God that we are able to recognize his voice and obey when he speaks. When we come together, it should consist of sharing of the overflow of the Lord in our lives with worship, praise, and celebration, springing forth as ministry to others and to our children. Children who grow up in a home where praise, prayer, and worship are part of the lifestyle they're accustomed to will probably be those children who love the Lord mightily. Why? Because this habit of praise, prayer, and worship is a lifestyle that has been exemplified in the home; and the most impressionable age a child can be shaped or molded is between the ages of one to five years old. During that time, a child learns and picks up new ideas quickly as they emulate their parents what they do and say. There are times when it seems that they're missing the mark, but you must teach them how to listen and recognize the voice of the Lord.

Deuteronomy 6:4-9 says, "And thou shalt love the Lord thy God with All thine heart, and with all thy soul, and with all thy might. And these words, which I command thee this day, shall be in Thine heart: And thou shalt teach them diligently unto thy children, and Shalt talk of them when thou sittest in thine house, and when thou liest Down, and when thou risest up. And thou shalt bind them for a sign upon thine hand, and they shall be as frontlets between thine eyes. And thou shalt write them upon the posts of thy house, and on thy gates."

We teach them through our actions and through our words. That kind of teaching is a dance itself, as we go through life showing forth the Lord in all our actions (a sign on our hands), and our attitudes (frontals over our foreheads) they will see and adopt our mannerisms. In Exodus 10:8 -11, God desires worship of the children. When a child is taught to pray as a child, how much easier would it be for him or her to pray when he becomes an adult? They need to minister unto the Lord.

Psalm 149:2-3 says, "Let Israel rejoice in him that made him: let the children of Zion be joyful in their King. Let them praise his name in the dance: let them sing praises unto him with the timbrel and harp."

It has been my experience that children can learn biblical concepts through music and movement. They love acting and role-playing, and when asked to play a certain part or character, the answer is almost always yes! Children are pliable and aim to please. God wants us to be that way also, that's why he says, "Except one becomes as a child he can not enter the kingdom." Humility from a child is true worship. Children give cheerfully and God loves a cheerful giver.

Psalm 100:4 says, "Give thanks to the Lord and bless his name." Thank God for the children and pray for them for they share an important part in his Kingdom.

Here's an exercise to try:

During Sunday school, have the children form a circle and sing a familiar song; make sure they know both the words and the meaning. As you teach them, allow the Lord to minister his love through them.

Breaking down barriers

Praise Is Victory's Cry

Praise until you see spiritually the walls of Jericho fall down! In chapter 6 of Joshua, it is stated: "Know the place where you are standing at this very moment is holy ground." Joshua 1:3 says, "That every place that the souls of our feet shall tread upon, that have I given unto you, as I said unto Moses."

God's blueprint has to be followed just as he says to Joshua, "I have already given you the city, the king thereof, and the mighty men of valor. And ye shall compass the city, [the word *compass* means "to encircle or surround"] and go around about the city once, for six days. And the priest shall bear before the ark seven trumpets of rams' horns: And the seventh day ye shall compass the city seven times, and the priest shall blow with the trumpets. And it shall come to pass, when they make a long blast with ram's horn, and when ye hear the sound of the trumpet, all the people shall shout with a great shout; and the wall of the city shall fall down *flat*, and the people shall ascend up every man straight before him." Pay close attention to the tenth verse: "And Joshua had commanded the people, saying, 'Ye shall not shout, nor make any noise with your voice, neither shall any word proceed out of your mouth, until the day I bid you shout; then shall ye shout,' and so it was, the people did as they were instructed."

I'm sure this was one of those times when you had to study to be quiet. The Bible says, "You shall decree a thing, and it shall be established." The word *decree* means you shall determine a thing, and it shall rise up; and on the seventh day, with the determined thing in mind, the people compassed the city seven times, and when the people did open their mouths, they shouted with a loud piercing sound. The sound was piercing enough to break down the walls of Jericho completely. Taken from the word *truwah*, a Hebrew word that means "a battle cry" or "an acclamation of joy, especially clang or trumpet as an alarum: alarm, blow(ing) of the trumpets, loud noise, taken from the root word *ruwa*, which means "to mar (especially by breaking)," figuratively "to split the ears (with sound)"—that is, shout for alarm or joy.

Can you imagine, God speaking to you, saying, "I'm going to give you a city. It's already yours, all I want you to do is walk around the city once for six days, and on the seventh day, I want you to cry aloud, saying, 'Spare not!' And the city is yours and everything in it." A word like that would have literally blown my mind! The fact that the Levites led the army in the war indicates to me that praise is a very powerful weapon. We don't understand the voice we have. It's a wind instrument, like a trumpet. I'm reminded in the book of Genesis when God called for Adam.

The Bible records that Adam heard the voice of the Lord walking in the cool of the day; I imagine the voice of the Lord sounding like thunder, causing you to tremble on the inside. That's just how powerful our voice is, especially when we're on one accord—same purpose, same mind—and saying the same things that God says. *Homologia*, or *homo*, which means "the same." Logia, or logos, which means "the written word." How forcible are right words? Which means, when we say what God says, we'll get the same results that God gets. Our words become like a hammer, nailing everything in place. Praise releases faith and breaks down the barriers in our lives.

The War Cry of the Warrior Is Authentic Praise

Saints, pick up your weapon; it's time to fight!

How to Recognize and
Manage Spiritual Time

Saints, it is vitally important that we understand the power of praise and worship. Praise is a knock on the door of heaven that announces unto the Lord our coming. He invites us in. He speaks in a small still voice that can only be heard with a quietness of the heart; therefore, we must not take for granted the opportunity we have to be visited by him.

We have in our churches today, people who just have to exit to go to the lavatory or to get a drink of water or something, and these things are done when praise and worship is in progress; this is when the pastor has to get up and say to the people, "Please, no walking or talking during the worship service." There is always a battle going on, the enemy does not want our praise to go forth, so he tries any and everything possible to cause that to happen. God has already given us the victory; but if we don't operate in knowledge of that truth, we will miss our blessing. As adults, we must improve on our attention span and teach our children how to listen, honor, and respect the voice of the Lord. Statistics show that the average attention span of an adult is about twenty minutes and a child less than that, which means that we must learn how to manage our time even on Sunday morning. Go to the lavatory before church starts, which is usually after Sunday school; at home, prepare your tithe and offering the night before, along with your clothing. This will expedite things on Sunday morning! My point is this: time management is vital. The Lord wants us to redeem the time. Work while it's day! On Sunday mornings, we are less self-conscious and more God-conscious. Like a sponge, we become porous and ready to absorb all that the Lord has for us, and our time is well spent. Enter the house with joyful expectations, shouting with a voice of triumph. Our prayer should be that we all come to repentance and do better. Become better people of Christ. Do battle in praise; praise gets you ready for worship. Songs like *Bless the Lord, Oh My Soul* (there's something about that name). Praise him because of who you are with songs that are directed to Jesus like *I'm Yours Lord, I Love You Lord.* Singing can cut through all types of principalities and strongholds when every word is pronounced clearly and profoundly, in the right key, and at the right time. Miriam understood the timing of God. Miriam placed Moses in the river at the right time in order for him to get into the right hands. Miriam was able to go with the flow.

Earlier, I spoke about the importance of seasons and timing. We must know when change has taken place. You cannot hang out with the girls or guys like you used to. When you find yourself unable to sleep at night when in time past you had no problem sleeping, that means God is stirring you and wants you to come away with him so that he can speak to you. This is called a change in prayer season. Another important fact is that we cannot allow anyone and everyone to beat the tambourine some sister or brother may have just gotten out of someone's bed, other than their own, and doing something out of order. They have no prayer life and they want to come into the house of God and beat the drums or play the piano or whatever; these instruments must be set aside for God's people, chosen and sanctified people. We must set the pace and flow. This is a season of order for spirituality. People want to be blessed and they want to see the move of God. They want something or someone to believe in and it is our responsibility as believers to lift up the name of Jesus through our daily activity of living. In order for the kingdom to grow and multiply, we must set the standards for those who are in darkness and encourage those who may be growing faint. Martin Luther King quoted, "If a man has not found something to live for, he is not fit to live." The Word of God puts it this way: a man who puts his hands on the plow and looks back is not fit for the kingdom. We must be living epistles of hope for those who are not yet fit for the kingdom, praying and always believing they will confess, believe, and receive the Lord and become fit for the master's use. Every believer must desire to live a life pleasing unto the Lord. Sometimes a consistent godly life is the only hope and witness to those who are in darkness. Live a life that is purpose filled to win souls. This is a season of witnessing. Every time we fail to do good when it's in our power, we sin against the Lord. Our daily prayer should be like that of King Solomon.

According to 2 Chronicles 6:19-42, we are covering an avenue of sin for ourselves as well as others, so that the response from the Lord in 2 Chronicles 7:12-21is "I have heard thy prayer, and have chosen this place to myself for an house of sacrifice and if my people which are called by my name, shall humble themselves and pray, and seek my face, and turn from their wicked ways: then will I hear from heaven, and forgive their sin, and will hear their land. Now my eyes are open and my ears attentive unto the prayer that is made in this place. I have chosen and sanctified this house that my name may be there forever: and my eyes and my heart shall be there perpetually, and if thy will obey me and do according to all that I have commanded thee, and observe my statutes and my judgments; I will establish the throne of thy kingdom."

We are his people and the sheep of his pastures; and as sheep, not knowing when or where to move, we must rely totally on the Lord, trusting in his Holy Word that if we ask anything in his name, he will do it. This is called a season of faith and trust. When we ask the Lord to touch, heal, deliver, make whole, renew, restore, revive, reconcile, regenerate, and mend the breaks in our hearts, in our relationships with our children and our churches, our marriages, and in so much more, we ask in faith. Romans 10:17 says, "Without faith it's impossible to please God." We have the power to conquer. Some of the needs mentioned above can be defined as walls in our lives; walls that need to be broken down flat. Once the walls fall down, we may even see where some things we credited as the work of the devil and all the while, God was using people, places, and things to set us up for victory.

Spiritual warfare

What is Spiritual Warfare?

Spiritual warfare is that continuing battle that we, as Christians, wage against our adversary, the devil. Satan, ole slew foot, along with his demonic forces, has from the beginning set to oppose the authority of God.

Ephesians 6:10-12 states, "Finally my brethren be strong in the Lord and in the power of His might. Put on the full armor of God, that you maybe able to stand firm against the wiles of the devil. For we wrestle is not against flesh and blood, but against principalities, against powers, against rulers of darkness of this world, against spiritual wickedness in high places."
"Satan is the god of this world and of the kingdom of darkness." (2 Cor. 4:4)

According to Colossians 1:13, Satan is totally opposed to the kingdom of God. He is now spiritual warfare cont;, concentrating all his efforts against the church. Satan is always seeking people whom he may devour. The Word records that he is as a roaring lion; that simply means his bark is worst than his bite. What should we as believers do? We must prepare ourselves for battle. Find out what the Word says and be strong, be in his might, and endure hardship as a good soldier.

Psalm 18:34-39 says, "The Lord will teach our hands to war."

Psalm 144:1 also states, "Blessed be the Lord, my rock, who trains my hands for war, and my fingers for battle."

What Are Some of the Things We Fight Against?

We cannot begin to name all the things we fight against, but we will name a few.

The wisdom of the world (James 3:14-16).

The world philosophies keep man from seeing the truth (Col. 2:8).

Deceitful spirits (1 Tim. 4:1-5).

False accusations (Rev. 12:10).

Sickness, deafness, dumbness, blindness, and violent nature

The fight is fixed!

Warfare Dance and Strongholds

What is Warfare?

Warfare is an armed conflict between enemies; a struggle.

What is Warfare Dance?

Warfare dance is an aggressive dance movement that is done to prepare the atmosphere for the preaching of the Word; these are usually sharp angular movements that are mighty to pull down strongholds.

Examples of warfare movements:

1. Sharp hand movements
2. Feet stomping
3. Kicks
4. Blows
5. Yelling
6. Running
7. Jumping
8. Struggle type movement
9. Walking

The Authority of the Feet

We have the power in our feet; to tread upon serpents and scorpions and over all the power of the enemy and nothing shall be any means harm you (Luke 10:19).

Every bit of ground that the sole of our feet shall tread upon God has given us to possess (Josh. 1:3).

And ye shall tread down the wicked; for they shall be ashes under the sole of your feet in the day I shall do this, saith the Lord of Hosts (Mal. 4:3).

"Come here put your foot on the neck of these Kings" (Josh. 10:24). To humiliate the enemy, one has to put his foot upon the captive's neck as Joshua's captains did. Romans 16:20 says, "The God of peace will soon crush Satan under your feet." As the dancers dance on to victory in the battle, the enemy stands defeated; the sole of the feet ends the battle. The enemy fears the feet in the war for they are truly a weapon.

With the determined thing in mind, we will gain the victory. Psalm 108:13 reminds us that "God will trample down our enemies."

Servants' Feet

"How beautiful are the feet of them that preach the gospel of peace, and bring glad tidings of good things!" (Rom. 10:15). As dancers, be prepared at all times to take the gospel wherever the Lord leads, whether in the community, or from one nation to another.

Be ready with whatever God tells you to do; just do it!

Protection of the Feet

I have kept my feet from every evil path so that I may obey your word (Ps. 119:101).

Walk not in the council of the ungodly (Ps. 1:1).

For thou has delivered my soul from death, mine eyes from tears, and my feet from falling (Ps. 116:8).

The word is lamp to my feet and a light unto my path (Ps. 119:105).

Then you will go on your way in safety and your foot will not stumble (Prov. 3:23, NIV).

The Word of God says that "he will make our feet like hinds feet and set us on high places.[Hands at war]: He teacheth my hands to war; so that a bow of steel is broken by my arm (2 Sam. 22:34-35).

What Are Hands Warring Against?

Spirit of depression, jealousy, oppression, and dismay, to name a few.

We have inner warfare in the mind. That's when the enemy tries to impregnate your mind with a lie; it starts with a thought!

Let this mind be in you that was also in Christ Jesus. (Phil. 2:5)

We also have inner warfare in the heart. Our heart has to be pure (Ps. 24:4).

God is able to do exceedingly, abundantly, above all we could ever ask or

think through the power that worketh in you (Eph. 3:20).

But, let us allow the peace of God to rule in our hearts (Col. 3:15).

We can defeat the enemy by pulling down strongholds.

What Are Strongholds?

Anything that has a tight grip upon us and is not easily shaken or changed is a
stronghold.

Here are some examples:

1. Fear

2. Uncleanness—nasty thoughts and gestures

3. Inordinate affection—uncontrollable desires

4. Malice—congealed anger

5. Filthy language—cursing, lying, and slander

6. Evil imagination

7. Anything that exalts itself against the knowledge of God

Sometimes, during a service, the Holy Spirit will lead you to go forth in dance to do warfare

in the spur of the moment. This is called "spontaneous dance." As the spirit gives you

utterance and direction, he will dance through you and create the steps as you go along.

When preparing for spiritual warfare one must dress for battle; "the whole armor of

God." (Eph. 6:10-20)

Put on the following:

1. The helmet of salvation

2. The breast plate of righteousness

3. Your loin's girt about with truth

4. Your feet shod with the preparation of the gospel of peace

5. The shield of faith to quench all the fiery darts of the enemy.

Let' focus on the shield of faith.

Shield of Faith

The shield of faith is a vital part of the Christian's armor. You are to put on the *whole armor of God* above all because the Christian life is a warfare; a spiritual conflict. As Paul names the different parts of the Christian's armor, he comes to the shield and emphasizes its importance by saying, "Above all taking the shield of faith," for with the shield of faith, nothing can hurt you; you are more than a conquerors through him (Rom. 8:37).

The importance of faith is seen in that

1. You cannot be saved without faith (John 3:36).

2. You cannot please God without faith (Heb. 11:6).

3. You cannot pray without faith (James 1:6).

4. You are to live by faith (Gal. 2:20).

5. You are justified by faith and not of works (Gal. 2:16).

6. Whatsoever is not of faith is sin (Rom. 14:23).

Who do we wage war against first?

The prince of the air

Spiritual Warfare Prayer

Father God, in the name of Jesus Christ of Nazareth, the Anointed One and His anointing, saturate us, minimizing our thoughts, will, and emotions. Enlarge yourself within us as only you can, until there is no more of us, but all of you. Send a cloud, a consuming fire, to burn all the chaff the people burdened down with. As your unseen hand move across this room, destroy every work of the devil, as we breathe out, "Satan, the Lord rebuke you and the blood of Jesus is against you. You are a defeated foe, and in all things we are more than conquers through him who love us." In Jesus's name. Amen!

Basic Terms

Fall Recovery

Your body can descend to the floor, as you release your body on the floor, you recover ascending slowly away from the floor by using proper technique; return to starting position. The movement can be swift or slow.

Marking

This movement, set to music, can be as we call it *three for nothing,* which means the time is off or suspended, or movement can be sustained, flowing, or sudden.

Traversing

This is moving across the floor from one side to another and not as diagonal.

Movement Level

This movement can be worked as high, medium, or low.

Contract

This movement may be used to express pain, or for holding on, or passion.

Improvise

This movement is made up as you go, depending on the message you want to send or express. It is to minister or perform without preparation.

Movement in Space

This movement is to transcend, move beyond, exceed, surpass, or to boldly go where no man has gone before; it's where you want go traveling, indirectly or just be there directly. A dancer can go anywhere his or her heart desires!

Format

This floor strategy for the dancers can be like a triangle, one line, or like coming from different directions. It can also be two rows as in a chorus, starting in cluster and opening to a sunburst; whatever format you choose, make sure it's not confusing. Make sure you send a clear picture.

Colors

Red .... Blood, passion, love, and authority

Blue .... Grace of God and peace

Green .... Growth, wisdom, knowledge, and wealth

Gold .... The anointing, as oil running down Aaron's beard

White .... Purity, holiness, righteousness; the Holy Spirit

Purple .... Royalty, adoption into royal priesthood

Black .... Death, sorrow, sin, mourning

Lavender .... Resurrection of Christ

Red, black, and white .... Can be used for crucifixion

Yellow .... Nonliturgical color, but can be used to add brightness

Burgundy .... Warrior

Silver .... Refiner's fire

These are just some of the colors and what they each represent, but there are many more. By using the color wheel, you can create beautiful colors that can enhance a dance piece and make it last in the eyes of the beholder. Understanding color can be very useful in choreography when preparing for production. The right choice of colors can be powerful.

My prayer for you as you read this book is that you will have a better understanding as it relates to dance, praise, and worship so that you're able to go forth in the ministry and understand the power and authority we have in these equipped temples. Always remember that the thoughts that God has toward you are good and not of evil. "Thoughts that will give you an expected end." (Jer. 29:11) My grandfather in Lord, Bishop Harvey D. Bryan, would always say, "Plan your work and work your plan."

Questions and Answers

1. What is a calling?

2. Who was the apostle called by God on the road to Damascus?

3. Name two ways a believer can fulfill the call in his or her life.

4. What is the aspect of worship?

5. What are the four key principles of prayer?

6. *Impartation*, what does it mean?

7. What is the root word for *praise*?

8. What is the root meaning of *Yadah*?

9. To flow as a dancer, what must one learn?

10. Name some of the ways we can turn up the heat in the worship service.

11. Name some acts of worship.

12. What is *marking*?

13. Define *movement in space*.

14. What is *traversing*?

15. What was the purpose of the priestly garment?

Colors and What They Represent

A. Green—

B. White—

C. *Red*—

D. *Yellow*—

E. *Burgundy*—

What is the title of this book?

Bibliography

Bergant, Kathleen Ann. *Communication Skills.* 1993

Blackaby, Henry. *Experiencing God.*

Brant, Roxanne. *Ministering to the Lord. 1973, 1993.*

Strong, James, *The New Strong's Complete Dictionary of Bible Words.*

Kohlenberger III, John R. Introduction by

Nelson, Thomas. *Vine's Complete Expository Dictionary of Old and New Testament Words.* Nashville, Tennessee: INC., 1984

Quest Study Bible, The. NIV Zondervan

Let the Children Come

Notes